May, 2008

Dear Destiny,

   You have many gifts
& talents. Develop them,
and I know you'll
   succeed!

                Love,
                Mrs. Cooper

D0455314

Maria Shriver as a little girl

Maria Shriver

JUST WHO
WILL YOU BE?

BIG QUESTION. LITTLE BOOK. ANSWER WITHIN.

HYPERION
New York

Library of Congress Cataloging-in-Publication Data
Shriver, Maria.
Just who will you be? : Big question, little book, answer within /
Maria Shriver.
p. cm.
ISBN: 978-1-4013-2318-9
1. Self-realization. 2. Self. 3. Individuality. 4. Meaning
(Philosophy) I. Title.
BJ1470.S52 2008
170'.44—dc22   2008002100

Hyperion books are available for special promotions and premiums. For
details contact Michael Rentas, Proprietary Markets, Hyperion, 77 West
66th Street, 12th floor, New York, New York 10023,
or call 212-456-0133.

Design by Fritz Metsch

FIRST EDITION

1   3   5   7   9   10   8   6   4   2

Dedication

This little book is dedicated to seekers of all ages.

May you always remember to trust your own heart,

listen to your own voice, and have the courage to

discover . . . Just Who You Will Be.

Acknowledgments

Just who I am has a lot to do with me, but it also has everything to do with the many people who have touched my life along the way—from my family to my circle of friends to the generous teachers who have shared themselves with me. You are my whole wide world, and I love you.

My one constant teacher has been my friend and mentor, Roberta Hollander. This book wouldn't have been possible without her love, her friendship, her wisdom, and her encouragement. She has taught me so much about life, and who I am has a lot to do with who she is.

Special thanks go to my agents, Jan Miller and Shannon Miser-Marven. This is our sixth book together, and I'm grateful to you both for your friendship, your confidence, and your plain old chutzpah.

To my new friends at Hyperion: Thanks for believing in the potential of this little book and for helping spread the message that who you are and who you will be has everything to do with your heart and your soul. I'm happy to be working with people who understand this message.

And very special thanks to Sandra Wareing and Teri Hess, who work with me every day, who keep me sane, and who help me in ways I'd need a whole separate book to explain.

Introduction

Not too long ago, I was whining to my teenage daughter. "I don't know what I want to be when I grow up!"

She took me by the shoulders, looked me dead in the eye, and said, "I hate to break it to you, Mom, but this is *it* for you! You *are* all grown up! You're cooked!"

I jumped out of my chair. "Not so!" I shot back. "You may think I'm over, but I'm not done yet! I'm still a work in progress, and I'm writing my next act now."

I told her, "You wait and see just who I will be!"

She rolled her eyes, turned up her iPod, and went off to find a saner person to talk to, like her little brother.

When she left, I wondered, "Is she right? Is this really it? *Am* I cooked? *Am* I over?"

Or do I get another shot at asking "What do I want to be when I grow up?"

Back when I was a kid, I spent a lot of time wondering just that: "What am I going to be when I grow up? What's my life going to be like?" I worried about it, because all my friends seemed sure about their futures. They wanted to be doctors, lawyers, teachers, politicians. Me, I didn't have a clue.

Then when I was sixteen, my dad ran for Vice President of the United States. (That's me at sixteen on the back of this book cover at the 1972 Democratic National Convention.) I was lucky enough to fly in the back of his campaign plane with all the working journalists—the ones who were asking all the questions and seemed to be having all the fun. Right then and there, I discovered what I wanted to be when I grew up: a TV journalist.

I wanted to be the woman on your television screen, telling you what was going on in the world, telling you what you needed to know. I wanted to be that smart, successful TV newswoman.

At first, I was too scared to tell anyone about my dream, worried that people would think I was crazy. After all, back then there weren't that many women on television. And I came from a family where everybody was in politics. So wanting to be a journalist was a weird choice, to say the least.

But after college, I set out to make my dream a reality anyway. I started at the bottom getting coffee and worked my way up to be a news producer, then a reporter, then a correspondent, then an anchor-woman. And I loved it. I just assumed I would be in TV news for the rest of my life. After all, that's who I *was*. That's what people called me: "TV newswoman Maria Shriver."

But sometimes life happens to you, and—bingo!—your idea of who you think you are just goes up in smoke. That's what happened to me.

One day out of nowhere, my movie-star husband announced he was running for Governor of California. Just sixty days later, he was elected. And because NBC News was worried that there might be a perceived conflict of interest between my news job and his political job, I was asked to resign.

Just like that my career was gone, and with it went the person I'd been for twenty-five years. And before you could say, "Toto, we're not in Kansas anymore!"— I became someone new, someone they called "the First Lady of the State of California."

"Say what?" I thought to myself. "The First Lady of the State of California? You've got to be kidding! That's not me! I didn't grow up wanting to be First Lady of *anything*!"

But there I found myself, and I didn't

have a clue what to do. And if that weren't enough of a shock, then this little incident just about pushed me over the edge:

I was out shopping in Santa Monica with my son. Along comes a guy handing out leaflets. He gives one to my son and then motions to me and says to him, "Are you with that woman?"

"Yep!" my son says.

The man asks, "Is she a model?" I give my hair a toss.

"Naaaah," my son says, looking over at me. "She's a housewife."

My neck snaps. My big beautiful movie-star glasses just about fly off my face. As the nice gentleman walks away, I grab my thirteen-year-old son's collar and shriek, "That man just asked you if I was a model, and you told him I'm a housewife?"

He says, "MOM! That's because you *are* a housewife!"

I'm still shrieking. "No, I am *not*, I am NOT! I'm a *journalist*!"

"*WERE* a journalist, Mom!" he shoots back.

And I snap right back at him: "I'm an author! I write books!"

Now he's digging in. "You're not writing any books *now*—*are* you, Mom?"

"Well, I'm a mother, for God's sake! A mother of four! You could have told him I'm a mother!"

"*Everyone's* a mother!" he says. "Face it, Mom! You don't have a *job!*"

I hate to admit it, but I grabbed him by his lapel and got in his face: "Listen, you!" I hollered. "*I am the First Lady of the State of California!*"

He rolls his eyes that awful way teenagers do and says, "Mom! I hate to break it to you. *Daddy* was elected, not you! Get used to it. You're a housewife!"

Talk about comeuppance. It didn't matter that I'd always trumpeted child-rearing and the work done at home as the most important job in our society, because I believe it is. But at that moment, I was shocked by my son's description of me, because for thirty years when I wrote something after the word "occupation," it was never the word "housewife."

Right about then, smack-dab in the middle of what felt like a world-class identity crisis, my nephew called to ask me to speak at his high school graduation.

"You've got to be kidding!" I bellowed at him. "How can I give you kids any words of encouragement when I'm struggling myself?"

Like any eighteen-year-old boy, he didn't hear me and just kept pressing on. He insisted I was the number-one choice of his senior class. I didn't believe him for a second, so I turned him down again.

He got creative. He said several presidential candidates had called begging to be the graduation speaker. He said various young movie stars had their publicists working the phones, trying to wangle an invitation. He said a certain real estate tycoon called and threatened to humiliate the entire senior class and their parents in the *Wall Street Journal* if *he* didn't get to speak at this graduation. None of it was true, of course, but he was trying to make his case.

He said, "See, Maria? You should be proud my class turned all of them down and picked you!" He's such a suck-up. But I held my ground.

So he did what any good Catholic

would do: he played the Guilt Card. I'm a sucker for guilt.

"Mar-EEEE-a!" he whined. "You're my one and only godmother! I'm only gonna graduate once! Don't you love me? Don't you care about me?"

So I caved.

Now, I've been giving speeches to audiences big and small for years, so you'd think this one would be the easiest thing in the world. But forget it. I went into a tailspin.

I couldn't for the life of me figure out what on earth these students wanted to hear from me. Did they want to hear from the Old Me or the New Me? And who was that? And what could I tell them? My own kids make sure I know that everything that comes out of my mouth is either boring or, worse, uncool, and that they know all of it already, anyway.

I stressed out trying to figure out what I could say. I ate licorice.

I stressed some more. I ate Dots.

I stressed out even more—and wiped out a bag of Swedish fish.

And then I wrote. I wrote in longhand on legal pads. I wrote in my room, in my office. I ripped it up, I threw it out. I wrote on the Lifecycle, on airplanes. Early in the morning and late at night. Starting over and over, driving myself nuts, trying to figure out exactly what these high school seniors expected to hear from me.

Finally I finished, and I was sure it would, as my son says, "suck."

But then on graduation day, I got a surprise. After I delivered the speech, people came up and urged me to turn it into a book, so they could remember it. And not just the kids. Parents also came up to say, "I wish I'd heard that message when I was a kid. And you know what? I needed to hear it now, too."

They all told me that what struck a chord with them was the question I'd posed in that graduation speech. It wasn't just "WHAT do you want to be when you grow up?" It was, "WHO will you be? WHO is the person you want to be? Who is the YOU you'll become? Who are *you*?"

And it turned out that writing that speech was a great thing for me, too, because it helped me redirect myself. It helped me get out of my tailspin.

Oh, not right away, because sometimes I'm a slow learner. But as time went on, as that question turned and churned inside of me, I began to answer it, learning a lot about myself in the process.

I've learned that asking ourselves not just *what* we want to be, but *who* we want to be is important at every stage of our lives, not just when we're starting out in the world. That's because, in a way, we're starting out fresh in the world every single day.

If we're headed in the wrong direction—or we're at a dead end on our path—or life throws us a curveball, as happened to me—asking ourselves that question can help get us on the right track.

And we very well might answer it differently in our twenties, in our thirties, in our forties, and beyond—which is where I am—and that's fine. We can allow ourselves to keep changing and growing and evolving. Actually, we're supposed to. And that's why the speech rang a bell with the adults that day, including me.

So here goes—the graduation speech I gave that wound up sending me off on a new road myself.

And stick around after you read the speech. I'll come back at the end of the book and tell you what I realized after I gave it.

"Just Who Will You Be?"

As I stand here before you, I wonder, "Why me? What could I tell you that your parents haven't already told you? What could I teach you that your teachers haven't already taught you? And what could I possibly share with you that your friends haven't already shared with you?"

I've been ripping my hair out trying to answer that question.

"Is it possible," I thought to myself, "that you want me to tell you what it's like being First Lady of the great state of California? Naaah, didn't think so.

"Aha!" I thought to myself. "Maybe you invited me because my husband is Arnold Schwarzenegger, and you want to know whether he still works out every day, now that he's Governor. Or maybe you want to know if he really misses being in the movies and making all that money. Naaah, if you wanted to know that stuff, you would have invited *him*."

Then I thought, "OK, maybe you invited me because I'm a Kennedy. You probably studied my uncles—President John Kennedy and Senators Bobby and Ted Kennedy—in history or social studies class, and you want to know what it was like growing up Kennedy."

But then I thought to myself, "No, no, no! It's the Shriver thing!" My nephew is in your class. You've heard that his grandpa, my dad, Sargent Shriver, started the Peace Corps, and my mom, Eunice, founded the Special Olympics. You want me to tell you what it was like growing up with Peace Corps volunteers crowded around the dinner table and Special Olympians doing back-flips in our swimming pool. But then I thought, "Nope, that doesn't feel right either."

So I figured, "OK! If it's not the First-Lady-Kennedy-Shriver-Arnold thing, it must be the television thing." You want to know what it was like to work at NBC

News with Katie Couric and Tom Brokaw. But none of us are at NBC News anymore, so that can't be it.

No, wait! I've got it! Maybe your parents made you invite me, because they want to know how a Democrat can stay married to a Republican for so many years. But hey! That's no speech. That's a book, and you're not getting that for free!

So finally, after making myself crazy, I asked my teenage daughter, "Why do you think this senior class wants me to be their graduation speaker?" She said, "Beats the heck out of me! All I know is if *my* school ever invited you, I'd be so mortified, I'd skip my own graduation!"

———

Bottom line: For the life of me, I couldn't figure out why you'd ask me to address you. And then this happened:

I went into Starbucks, like I do every morning to get my three shots of espresso over ice—hey! I've got four kids—and this woman comes up to me all excited.

"Miss Kennedy!" she says. "Oh, I mean, Miss Kennedy Shriver," she stammers. "Oh—no! I mean *Mrs*. Kennedy Shriver Schwarzenegger! Uh, I mean, Mrs. Governor. Oh, sorry, no no no! I mean Mrs. First Lady—oh, my God!"

She's now beside herself. She says, "I'm sorry, I'm sorry! It's just that it's all such a mouthful!"

I say, "Yeah, tell me about it!"

She's still stammering. She says, "I don't know *what* to call you!"

I try to calm her down. So I say, ever-so-gently, "Please. Just call me Maria."

So the woman chills out, takes a deep breath, and says, "OK, Mrs. Kennedy Governor. I just want you to know that I love you. I love your whole family. I've been following you and them for years—and I've read all your books. And I've always wanted to meet you—just so I could ask you *one thing*!"

"What's that?" I ask.

She leans close to me and whispers: "What . . . is it like . . . to be friends . . .

with someone . . . as famous . . . as OPRAH?"

All of a sudden, it dawned on me. That's *it*! It's the fame thing! I can talk to you about the fame thing!

I realize I'm standing here today because people know who I am. I have some measure of what we call "fame." Some of it I was born into—some of it I earned—some of it came through marriage—and some of it comes just from knowing the people I know.

In fact, a recent survey of kids your age revealed that the thing your generation wants more than anything else in the world is to be famous, period.

"Now, why is that?" I wondered. What is it about fame that makes it so alluring— so desirable? What's the attraction? What does it really mean? Not just to the person who's famous, but to the people drawn to him or her. After all, in the last several years, we've seen so many people become famous for—what? For just being famous!

Think about it. Consider some of those famous young women who get their picture taken every single day getting in and out of cars, going out to lunch, or shopping. What have they done to justify their fame? Anything? Or the person whose little video is on YouTube for a minute.

Even the people who *lose* on *American Idol* become famous, for God's sake.

These people hire publicists to push their names and images onto the hundreds of cable channels and magazines and websites that are screaming for fresh material every day. So as a result, we're bombarded with their pictures and stories 24/7. Before you can say "Andy Warhol," they're famous!

And on top of that, they make it seem so rewarding, so easy. Famous people always seem to look happy. They always look rich. They always look thin. If they happen to be fat, they'll be thin next week. Famous people seem to have it all. So I can sort of understand why many young people might have fame as their main goal in life.

But let me say, for whatever it's worth—and since I'm kind of famous, it might be worth something—fame *isn't* a goal worthy of your life.

It's true, fame can get you a good table in a restaurant. It can get you a hot date with someone who's attracted to fame. If you're lucky, it can also make you rich and powerful. And if you're really lucky, it can get you invited to be a graduation speaker.

But no matter how good fame looks on the outside, it's just an image. Trust me: Just because people know your name, it doesn't mean they know who you are.

Believe it or not, fame in and of itself can't make you happy. It can't make you feel worthy. It can't give you a life of meaning and joy. That, I've learned, is strictly an inside job.

Now, what do I mean by "an inside job"? I mean that the only way you can come to feel worthy, and really good about yourself—the only way to find a life of meaning and joy—is to find your own voice, find your own path, follow your own heart, and live your own life, not an imitation of somebody else's.

Now I know this isn't the easiest thing

to do, because we live in a world that seems to put a premium on the external trappings of fame. But figuring out who you are, finding your own passion, ful-filling your own dreams—now *that's* a goal worthy of your life. And might I say that the people I've met who are happiest in their lives—famous or not—have done just that.

But let's just say for a minute you're sitting there thinking, "Easy for *her* to say! She's already kind of famous. I want to know what that feels like! I want to be famous, too!"

Okay, so if that's the case, let me tell you that I think it's important to ask yourself this: What do you want to be famous *for*?

When you try to answer that question, please set your sights high—because you can be famous for doing something great in this world, something that matters, something that makes life better.

You can use your fame to inspire people and give them hope. I think now more than ever we need famous people with integrity, character, and vision— people who want to lead, who want to change the world and make it a more peaceful, hopeful, and compassionate place, a place where more people feel accepted and valued for who they are.

You know, many years ago, my father gave a college graduation speech where he told the students, "Allow me to challenge you not to think so much about what you will do or where you will go. Allow me to challenge you to think about . . . what you believe."

In other words, he was challenging them to look at what they *believe*, in order to find out who they could *become*.

In truth, that's the most important question we can all ask ourselves throughout our lives: "What do I believe— and who do I want to be?" Answering that question is crucial, because what you believe is the foundation upon which you build yourself as you continue to grow.

Now I know all this might sound a little heavy, so I thought I'd lighten things up. I've written my message into a poem especially for you on this important day in your life. My son thinks it sounds like a prehistoric rap lyric.

Even if it does, I hope it will encourage you to think about the unique person who you and *only* you are turning into.

The poem is called . . . "Just Who Will You Be?"

Congratulations!
The day has come
The tests are over
The future's begun

It's a little bit scary
Exciting, too
To go out in the world
And find out . . . Who is you!

And that's what will happen
Now that high school is done
You'll be figuring out
Your place in the sun

So here's what I'm asking

And you ask it, too:

JUST WHO WILL YOU BE?

That's the question for you

When you look in the mirror

It's an image you see

But down deep inside

JUST WHO WILL YOU BE?

Will you follow the crowd

Or follow your gut?

Will you be a leader

Or anything but?

When you go to college

You'll want to belong

That doesn't mean doing

What you know is wrong

Be honest and ethical

When temptation calls

Don't take the shortcut

That leads to a fall

Who wants to belong

To a group that seems "rad"

But does things that make you

Feel lonely and bad?

You have a mind

And you know how to think

You don't *have* to do something

That really does stink

Tell yourself, "I don't need it!

No matter to me!

That isn't the me

That I want to be!"

And while you figure out

Just what you want to do

You'll be figuring out

Who the "who" is in you!

Now, something you'll learn

As you go on in school

Is that you can be kind

At the same time you're cool

It's cool to be nice

I once heard Bill Gates say:

"Be nice to a nerd,

He'll be your boss someday!"

And you will attract all the

Best friends on earth

By being a trustworthy

Person of worth

As you go down the road

As you see what you see

You'll keep right on learning

JUST WHO YOU WILL BE

Everyone's life

Is an uncharted course

So go out and live it

Without regret or remorse

Take time to be quiet

Hear what your own voice is

Learn who you are

By making good choices

You can get the cool clothes

And the jewelry and car

But that doesn't measure

The person you are

Not the things you collect,

Though all of it's nice

If you worship belongings

You'll pay a big price

The price that you'll pay

Is expensive, you'll see

It's becoming the person

You won't want to be

Buried under belongings,
And choking on "stuff"
Someone so unhappy
'Cause there's never enough

And if you measure your worth
By the clothes you have on
What happens when all of your
Booty is gone?

So here is my question
And you ask it, too
JUST WHO WILL YOU BE?
It's a biggie for you

Now don't think I'm saying

You won't make mistakes

That's just part of living

That growing up takes

Sometimes you'll feel lonely

Sometimes you'll feel lost

If you want to achieve

Sometimes that's the cost

As you go down one road

And don't like what you find

Remember it's OK

To just change your mind

And don't be so fearful
You're too scared to fail
I've had my share of failures
And lived to tell the tale

If you don't stick your neck out
You'll be safe, it's true
But you also won't find out
Who is the real you

Doing only what's easy
Won't break you a sweat
But you also won't learn
Lessons you need to get

The lessons will teach you

What you need to know

To find out who you'll be

And which way you'll go

And when it comes time

To pick your career

Start at the bottom

And work up with no fear

It's the way that I did it

It's the best way to learn

Be humble and patient

A big salary you'll earn

Who you work for and with
Is important, it's true—
Can be even more crucial
Than what you actually do

So try to find someone
Who'll serve as your mentor
I had such a person
I believe that God sent her

This is the person
Who'll guide you and teach you
So keep your ears open
And let mentors reach you

And from my experience
Here's a piece of advice:
I thought workaholism
Was ideal and nice!

As you do your career
Don't do what I did
By working too much
And not being a kid

Be playful and joyous
And take time to breathe
'Cause it isn't your job
That defines who you'll be

So here's that same question

Coming right back at you

JUST WHO WILL YOU BE?

That's the question for you

But always remember

That who you will be

Will be up to you

Not your Mom, Dad—or me!

And speaking of parents:

They've done so much work

To get you to here

So don't be a jerk!

Treat them with kindness

And have some compassion

Even if they don't like

Your teenager fashion!

Talk to them, e-mail them

No whining allowed

Let them know how you're doing

Let them be proud!

Once again I am asking

And you ask it, too

JUST WHO WILL YOU BE?

The main question for you

When you answer the question
Don't think just of fame
Think of your precious legacy
Think of your name!

When you ask, "Who am I
And who will I be
And just exactly how long
Will it take to be me?"

I say, "Please take your time
Don't be in a rush
Take time to consider
And ponder and such"

Will you be a person
Who's running on greed?
Or will you be the one giving
To people in need?

Will you just collect awards
To put on your shelves?
Or will you help people
Who can't help themselves?

'Cause when I feel lousy
Or lost or I'm nervous
I feel better about me
When I am of service

Think of using your brains
And your talent and youth
To solve difficult problems
To find out the truth

To make this crazy world
A far better place
To make some improvements
For our human race

Think of raising great children
Or creating great art
Helping out in communities
Sharing your heart

And if you are so lucky

That the things that you do

Attract you some fame?

Well, "God bless" to you!

But don't get confused

And be clear-headed, too

You aren't your fame

And your fame isn't you!

Fame's just a perception

An image, a role

But it isn't the truth

And it isn't your soul

Under the spotlight
The shine fades real fast
And the fun of the fame
Never really does last

There are folks who are famous
But their lives are a mess
Because just being famous
Doesn't bring happy-ness

Take away all the sparkle
The glitter and such
And who is the person
You admired so much?

You yourself will discover

That you are much more

Than your job or your group

Or the babe you fought for

So it's not on the outside,

The things you can see—

It's the stuff on the inside

That shows who you'll be

Now a word to young women:

Please don't lose yourself

You don't *need* anyone

To be someone yourself!

You can be girly *and* strong

Have careers and go far

And when you get married

Not lose who you are

And you young men in the room?

Know this from the start

You can be manly *and* macho

And still have a warm heart

Now what about love

And what about sex?

I leave that for the end

For the biggest effects

My advice to you here:

Don't go off the deep end!

Don't rush to get married

When you do, pick a friend!

'Cause when all of the steam

Cools off, and it will,

You'll have someone to laugh with

And you'll love them still

So I asked it before

And here's one more time

JUST WHO WILL YOU BE

When you get to prime time?

In the end all that matters

Is not in the bank

Not your money or home

Or the gas in your tank

It not just about

Your husband or wife

It's what's in your heart

How you live your own life

How much joy do you give?

How much love, how much laughter?

All the people you helped

And felt so good after

It's the last time I'll ask it

On this big day for you:

JUST WHO WILL YOU BE?

That's the question for you

If you follow your heart . . .

And just listen to me

You'll turn into the you . . .

You are *destined to be!*

Lessons Learned

Now, when I came home after giving that speech, I told a dear friend how I'd agonized and tortured myself trying to figure out in advance who those students expected me to be and what they wanted me to say.

I had told them that fame wasn't the answer. I had told them "the only way to find a life of meaning and joy is to find your own voice, find your own path, follow your own heart, and live your own life, not an imitation of somebody else's."

But then it hit me over the head. In

worrying myself to death about what those students wanted from me, I wasn't heeding my own message! I realized I was still looking to others to tell me who I should be, instead of answering the question for myself.

My friend said to me, "Maria, you have a choice. You can spend the rest of your life trying to measure up, trying to figure out and then fulfill other people's expectations of you—or right now, you can make a decision to let all that go. And you can start by talking about what *you* know, what *you* feel, and what *you* think. You can start talking about just who *you* want to be!"

WHOA! Me?

For this people-pleasing, legacy-carrying, perfection-seeking Good Girl, that was a news bulletin—because that's exactly what I'd been struggling with for the past few years.

As I mentioned in the beginning, I felt like I'd lost who I was when I'd lost my job. In my mind, I'd even lost my name, because after all, when people came up to me in the street all excited now, they'd ask me, "Aren't you Somebody? Aren't you famous? Aren't you the Kennedy who's married to the Governor?" And I wanted to scream, "Hey, I'm ME! I'm MARIA!"

After all the years I'd struggled to make a name for myself—traveling all over the world, chasing news stories, scoring big interviews, writing best-selling books, winning accolades and awards—people didn't seem to know who I was anymore. And the truth is, I'm embarrassed to say, I allowed that to chip away at my self-worth.

I felt like a shadow of myself. And I found myself wondering on more than a few occasions, "If I'm not that news-woman on TV anymore, who am I?"

Then I had a flash. If I could just get my old TV news job back, I'd regain my footing. I'd be myself again. I wouldn't feel so lost. I'd have a real job, so I'd have a real identity.

Maria would exist again—in your eyes, and in mine. I'd know who I was, because *you* did.

So I called NBC to convince them they should make me a correspondent again. And—lo and behold!—they agreed.

My old job! My old salary! My old friends! My old ME! Yippeeee! The plan was to go back to work as soon as my husband was reelected.

But then something happened. I stood up at my husband's inauguration and recited a Hopi Prayer that I'd come across in a book.

It goes like this:

We have been telling the people that

  this is the eleventh hour

Now we must go back and tell the

  people that this IS the Hour.

Here are the things that must be

  considered:

Where are you living?

What are you doing?

What are your relations?

Where is your water?

Know your garden.

It is time to speak your truth.

In the days that followed, I read that prayer over and over again. Those questions resonated deep inside of me—and I struggled to try to answer them.

So before I went back to work, I decided I'd go away by myself for a couple of days.

I'd never done that before in my whole life—so busy had I been, running around upholding the Shriver legacy with my good works and public service—helping my husband build his legacy with his movies and politics—being part of the NBC legacy with my high-profile interviews and journalism awards—and living the Kennedy legacy with my teeth and my hair.

It was so out of character for me to go away alone that my daughter asked me if I was going to rehab!

But off I went, and I was scared.

I went to a beautiful place, and I sat. I thought. I breathed. And I asked myself, "If this is the hour—how *do* I want to spend it? What *do* I want to do with it? Do I really want to go back to the TV news business—and if so, why? Do I want to try to churn out another best seller—and if so, why? Do I want to try to be the best First Lady California's ever seen—and if so, why? If it's time to speak my truth, what *is* my truth?"

All I got were more questions.

And then when I came home, I started really paying attention to what was on television news these days. It seemed to be all about actors overdosing and former sports stars getting in trouble and actresses getting DUIs. I knew deep down that when I went back to work, those would be the kinds of stories I'd be doing, too. It made me realize that the news business had changed—and so had I.

So I picked up the phone, called NBC, and said, "I'm not coming back."

My friends were horrified! My lawyer and agent even more so. Everyone in my life screamed, "Oy vey! *Now what? What are we going to do with her?*"

My girlfriends rushed into action.

"How about starting your own book imprint? How about starting your own major online media company? How about joining some big fancy corporate boards? You could always do a hair commercial!"

But for some reason, none of it felt right. For the first time in my life, I had no plan of action. And where *I* come from, that's a big no-no.

You see, I was raised in a family that equated self-worth with personal achievement. Achievement brought not just acceptance, but power, recognition, and love.

I'd been taught that if you weren't

doing, if you weren't serving, if you weren't accomplishing and accomplishing big—then you really weren't being. You weren't even seen.

I felt that overachievement was expected of me. That's the way my parents and my family had lived their lives—and they had changed the world.

So with no new high-profile goal of my own, I was in uncharted waters. I had been living a life of privilege, power, and fame – filled with all the excitement, glamour, and high drama people dream of—but now when I stood still, I felt empty. And that scared me to death.

For me, it was a moment of truth to

realize deep in my soul that the old solutions—the external fixes that had motivated me for so long—just didn't work for me anymore. It shocked me, and it shook me to my core. And that sent me on an inward journey to answer the question: Just who *did* I want to be?

When I reflected on that question, I realized I'd been answering it wrong my whole life. I'd always answered it with my resumé. But the true answer, I saw, is about my heart, my values, and my soul. *Who* I am, not *what* I am.

It isn't really about others' perceptions and expectations of me either, even though we all worry about that.

We worry, "Am I fulfilling my parents' expectations of me?" "What will my friends think of the school I'm going to?" Later on we worry, "Will they like the person I fell in love with?" and "Will people be disappointed with my career choice?" And then it's "What will others think of the way I'm raising my kids?" Or "What will they think if I decide *not* to have kids? Or decide *not* to get married? What if I gain weight or show signs of aging?"

Well, I now see that who we are has nothing to do with any of that outside stuff. What I've learned on this journey is that I have worth as a human being—not just because of the job I have or the resumé or how I look or who I married or the family I was born into. I've learned we're all worthy of being loved just for being ourselves.

I've also learned it's OK to change. Sometimes it's not just OK, but mandatory. You *can* let go of some beliefs that maybe have served you well along the way, but just don't work for you anymore. We're *supposed* to grow and evolve. We have to give ourselves the permission and freedom to stay open to change.

I'm not talking about running away or having plastic surgery or a dye job. I'm not talking about throwing away our core principles and values and morals. I'm talking about exactly the opposite. I'm talking about letting life's experiences affect you and mature you. I'm talking about going down deep and finding out where you're at and where you need to go next.

And it's not just losing a job that can ignite the process of change, as it did for me. Life intervenes in many ways. People close to us pass away. New friends come into our lives. We go off to college or graduate school or move to another city. Children grow up and leave. Or our interests change, and we want to learn something new. We might remember old dreams and goals we once had and decide it's time to work toward them. Or we're just plain stuck and need something different to jump-start our lives.

That's the time to unwrap the person you are and ask the question: "Just who will I be?"

I now realize that everyone I've ever met in my life who's interesting, who has a life of deep meaning and joy, is still open to new answers to that question, new opportunities for change and growth.

And it doesn't have to be a cataclysmic shift on the outside. It can be a seismic shift on the inside. Signing up for school on the Internet. Refocusing on your health and doing something real about it. Beginning and sticking with a spiritual practice. Committing to sitting quietly with yourself twenty minutes a day to see what you learn.

The change doesn't have to be huge, but it may have to be deep. A deep change for me was realizing I'd have to take the time to know what I *feel*, in order to know who I am and who I want to be.

That was a huge awakening for me, because I was always taught to power right *past* what I was feeling—to "buck up, get a grip, and carry on." And the fact is, that attitude did help me achieve a lot in my life. After all, if you don't feel your fears, you're fear-less! But it didn't help me know who I was.

The truth is I've always felt that "who I was"—my personal story—was written and preordained before I lived it. That's why I was always scrambling to live up to the myth, always worried others would think I wasn't fulfilling my role.

I now realize that's no way to live.

Many of you may also feel that you're scrambling to fulfill your roles in every-body's life but your own. You may feel you're not entitled to show up as anyone but the perfect student, the perfect son or daughter, the perfect spouse or partner, the perfect employee or parent.

You may believe you're not allowed to think of yourself as separate from your job, your family, and all the other legacies you inhabit.

But what I've come to understand is that we are first and foremost human beings in our own right. We're entitled to our own lives, our own dreams and goals, our own legacies.

I've finally learned after all these years that I don't need to define myself with a certain job or a certain name or a certain role in order to tell myself who I am. I've learned that all my roles are simply a *part* of me—but they're not *all* of me.

I've learned that by looking at myself

apart from my roles—by softening and taking off some of the armor I put on as a child and wore my whole life—I can more clearly see and feel the people around me. Now that I'm not so obsessed about whether I measure up to other people's expectations, I've found a new gentleness and kindness in myself, *for* myself and for others.

What matters most to me now is what *I* expect of myself. What matters most to me now is that I *know* myself—what my heart feels, what my inner voice is telling me.

So just who am I?

Well, I've been amazed to discover that inside that tough, dutiful, responsible girl who always worried about what everyone else was thinking and always "got with the program"—why, there's actually a free-spirited, adventurous, and creative person inside.

After my hard-charging, competitive life, I've been amazed to discover I'm actually a nurturing and spiritual person who seeks joy, peace, and meaning in her life.

That's who I am.

And Just Who Will I Be?

I'll be Maria, but not the same Maria

with the same motivations I had in my twenties or my thirties or my forties. And that's a good thing.

I will feel my way into who I am becoming.

I will continue to work on issues that are important to me—like trying to give a hand to help people out of poverty and shining a light on extraordinary things women are doing all over this country. I will continue to be of service in my community, because that helps give my life meaning.

I will continue to live the faith I say I have, because I've learned that when I do, it can actually sustain me.

I will continue to encourage my family to discover and pursue their own passions.

I will continue to pass along my life's lessons, because that gives me joy. Remember: You are the only person on this planet with your story. What's the point of being here unless you share it, pass it on, and help somebody else?

I will try to help my aging parents deal with infirmity and live with dignity because that gives me peace.

I will figure out what my own next job will be, and go do it.

But most important, I will try to live an authentic life that feels true to me— which means living life as myself, not an imitation of anyone else, and not the reflection of myself in anyone else's eyes.

Above all, I will be a work in progress, because when I told my daughter, "I don't know what I want to be when I grow up," I really meant it.

And I will write another book when I figure all this out.

In other words, I am not cooked! But I am unfinished, and I hope when you get to be my age, you will be, too.

Meantime, *who* I'll be is up to me. Same as it is for you.

Maria, meet Maria.

THE END

Oh! And one more thing . . .

Not too long ago, I came up with a list of Ten Things I Pledge to Myself, in order to keep myself focused and centered on just who I want to be. I introduced this Pledge at the California Governor and First Lady's 2007 Conference on Women, in Long Beach, California. I'm sharing it with you with the hope you may enjoy coming up with your own pledge to yourself. But please write it in pencil—because just like you, it's bound to change.

And remember: Enjoy the ride!

My Pledge

1. I pledge to "show up" in my life as myself, not as an imitation of anyone else.

2. I pledge to avoid using the word "just" to describe myself. For example, I won't say, "I'm just a mother," "I'm just a student," or "I'm just an ordinary person."

3. I pledge to give myself ten minutes of silence and stillness every day to get in touch with my heart and hear my own voice.

4. I pledge to use my voice to connect my dreams to my actions.

5. I pledge to use my voice to empower myself and others.

6. I pledge to serve my community at least once a year in a way that will benefit other people.

7. I pledge to ask myself, "Who am I? What do I believe in? What am I grateful for? What do I want my life to stand for?"

8. I pledge to sit down and write my own mission statement.

9. I pledge to live my own legacy.

10. And I pledge to pass it on.

Your Pledge

1. _____

   _____

2. _____

   _____

3. _____

   _____

4. _____

   _____

5. _____

   _____

6. _____

   _____

7. _____

   _____

8. _____

   _____

9. _____

   _____

10. _____

    _____

Photo of Maria Shriver by Katherine Schwarzenegger

Remember: Just who you will be is up to you.